DYLAN VAN DEN BERG is a Palawa writer and dramaturg. He has held residencies at Sydney Theatre Company through the Emerging Writers Group, at Griffin Theatre Company through the Studio Artist program, and was a participant in ILBIJERRI's BlackWrights program. His plays include *Whitefella Yella Tree* (Griffin Theatre Company), *Milk* (The Street Theatre), *Ngadjung* (Belco Arts), *The Camel* (Motley Bauhaus/FlickFlickCity), *All that Glitters is Not Mould* (NIDA), *The Chosen Vessel* (Early Phase: The Street Theatre) and *The Flood* (National Theatre of Parramatta). He is a two-time recipient of the Nick Enright Prize for Playwriting at the NSW Premier's Literary Awards, one time winner of the VIC Premier's Award for Drama, and was shortlisted for the UK's Bruntwood International Award for Playwriting. He studied theatre at the ANU and the State University of New York.

# milk

Dylan Van Den Berg

**CURRENCY PRESS**
The performing arts publisher

CURRENCY PLAYS

First published in 2021
by Currency Press Pty Ltd,
Gadigal Land, Suite 310, 46–56 Kippax Street, Surry Hills, NSW 2010,
Australia
enquiries@currency.com.au
www.currency.com.au

in association with The Street

This revised edition first published in 2023.

Copyright: *Introduction* copyright © Dylan Van Den Berg, 2023; *Milk* copyright © Dylan Van Den Berg, 2021, 2023.

COPYING FOR EDUCATIONAL PURPOSES
The Australian *Copyright Act 1968* (Act) allows a maximum of one chapter or 10% of this book, whichever is the greater, to be copied by any educational institution for its educational purposes provided that that educational institution (or the body that administers it) has given a remuneration notice to Copyright Agency (CA) under the Act.
For details of the CA licence for educational institutions contact CA,
12/66 Goulburn Street, Sydney, NSW, 2000; tel: within Australia 1800 066 844 toll free; outside Australia 61 2 9394 7600; fax: 61 2 9394 7601; email: memberservices@copyright.com.au.

COPYING FOR OTHER PURPOSES
Except as permitted under the Act, for example a fair dealing for the purposes of study, research, criticism or review, no part of this book may be reproduced, stored in a retrieval system, or transmitted in any form or by any means without prior written permission. All enquiries should be made to the publisher at the address above.

Any performance or public reading of *Milk* is forbidden unless a licence has been received from the author or the author's agent. The purchase of this book in no way gives the purchaser the right to perform the play in public, whether by means of a staged production or a reading. All applications for public performance should be addressed to the author c/- Cameron's Management, tel: +61 2 9319 7199, email: info@cameronsmanagement.com.au

Cover design by Jenna Lee for Currency Press.

Currency Press acknowledges the Traditional Owners of the Country on which we live and work. We pay our respects to all Aboriginal and Torres Strait Islander Elders, past and present.

A catalogue record for this book is available from the National Library of Australia

# Contents

*Introduction*
  *Dylan Van Den Berg* vii

MILK 1

*Roxanne McDonald and Dylan Van Den Berg in The Street Theatre's* Milk, *2021 (Photo: Creswick Collective)*

# Introduction

My great-grandmother's shell necklace sits on my desk, its pearlescent surfaces glinting whenever I'm writing—spurring me on when I'm feeling lost and flashing coldly at me when I'm feeling lazy. It has me thinking about all the hands that've held it—felt the chill of green maireener shells on their palm. It has me thinking of the knowledge, passed down and down and down, that brought it into being. And it reminds me of the power of our storytelling culture—of sharing stories which are birthed into 'now', but which have trickled through time—through the fingers of ancestors—and which will eventually fall into the palms of those who come down the line.

The fragments of *Milk* fell into my palms over a long period of time—bits and pieces from family who shared knowledge and reflections on what it is to be Palawa as they grew up, or yarns about ancestors from long ago—and, importantly, the kind of future they imagined for themselves. It was a gift to grow up around my great-grandmother, who was born on Flinders Island, where she lived for much of her childhood. Life there was at once hard—our family lived in a house made of flattened kerosene tins that whistled in the wind—and freeing; there was mutton bird season, and the joy of family squeezed into every inch of every home, and they were raised by a glorious assortment of Aunties and, of course, Gran's own nan, Ellen Smith. The memories that survived—that were the most easily drawn from my Gran as she reached her nineties—were those of a childhood spent in the embrace of a loving community. What she remembered most, looking back from the wise old age of 93? The taste of mutton-bird, and the voice—mostly soft but with a bite when the situation called for it—of her grandmother.

The cold and the wet and the poverty came later in her recollections, almost afterthoughts to an early life saturated with stories, collecting shells along the shoreline and looking to the sky for a sign of what tomorrow might bring.

And then things changed. Our family moved to mainland Tasmania, where their childhood joy was considered primitive—where their stories, passed down and lived by, were scoffed at. Where those with skin shades darker than white were violently excluded. My Gran experienced 'otherness' for the first time and retreated into her family and into herself. It wasn't safe to be an 'islander' in the context of 1930's Tasmania, and so our family tried to melt away and forget. There's great privilege in being able to hold onto the past, in anchoring oneself to an identity; to be Blak at that time was to forgo decently paid employment, to be segregated at the pub—to fight for your country but receive nothing in return. Racism lurked everywhere.

A meeting of the past and the future birthed this play: I had a baby on the way, and my Gran was in her final years. Where would the stories go? How do I make sure my daughter knew where she came from—who she came from—and all that it meant? How do I put onto the page all the feelings I carried around in my chest and my brain—the anger and the pride and the confusion and the fear about a future with a young person to guide and without an Elder to guide me?

*Milk* is an act of collective memory, as well as a personal exploration of Blakness. I was deeply honoured to work closely with my Aunty Gaye Doolan on the play. She encouraged rigour and told me when I got things wrong; her generosity lives in every part of this work. The play asks a knotty question of its audience: who gets to be Blak? It asks us to consider the history of this place we call Australia, and to grapple with colonial legacies of violence and oppression. Whitefellas have ripped stories away from us for centuries in the name of 'progress', and the reclamation of yarns and Dreaming is an ongoing project.

And this question—or series of questions, I guess, around identity and cultural legacy—applies as much to Blackfullas. Our own mobs have turned on each other, tearing away at the lived experience of brothers and sisters and cousins and countrymen, gatekeeping something that can't be quantified or neatly drawn up in the way some would like. What's the 'right' amount of culture to learn? How many stories make you Blak? Who do you need to grow up with to solidify your connection? And who benefits from the exclusion of mob? It emerges from trauma and pain—from the disappointments of the colonial project—but it manifests as violence, both inward and clumsily directed at those who are piecing together the reality of their lives. Culture, like love, is not a finite resource.

Fundamentally, *Milk* is a memory play, where characters' recollections lead to deeper self-knowledge. As their memories begin to bleed and blur, the true 'holder' of the memory is less important than who hears it; character C must witness the zig and the zag of A's life to understand her spirit—and he must draw out of B the devastating reality of her situation to finally forgive her. All three characters are part of something bigger—more than an act of collective memory, their yarns are laying the foundation for the future of C's unborn daughter. The play imagines a better future for those to come, and calls for a more restful past for the Old Ones to nestle into.

The first part of the play that I wrote were A's final lines. With the full story of my ancestor playing out before me, I wondered how she might want to the story to end: what does she get, when it's all said and done? She'd been battered and sold and commodified and abused. But she'd also been a mother, a grandmother, a dancer—stood up and moved her black body in defiance of whitefellas. And she'd had to exist in the cruelty of two distinct worlds: one that valued her, and one that demonstrably did not.

What could I gift her, way down the line?

Some quiet. Some peace. Somewhere she could exist on her own terms. Not the end of something, but the start.

When my Gran passed away, just shy of her ninety-sixth birthday, and a few months after the premiere of this play, it felt like a hundred stones had rained down on my chest. I cried and I held my daughter, who was two years old. I cried about the end, and I cried about the beginning. And when I un-scrunched my eyes, my brain rung off an inventory of her life: a Blak world and a white world, three children, countless grandchildren and great-grandchildren (and one chubby-legged great-great grandchild, who she delighted in holding), thousands of meals cooked and plated for eager mouths, countless hugs and floral hankies pulled from her sleeve, applied to the salty-snotty faces, the sting of losing a daughter and a son, the autonomy of driving an aqua Holden Barina around Devonport well into her eighties, an absent father driven away because his dark skin meant nowhere was safe, the thrill of a perfect cuppa. What my Gran got—what she earned, right at the end—was some quiet.

Like her ancestors before her, she got some peace.

At last, she got that.

*Dylan Van Den Berg*
*Ngunnawal Country*
*September 2023*

*Roxanne McDonald in The Street Theatre's* Milk, *2021 (Photo: Creswick Collective)*

*Milk* was first produced by The Street at The Street Theatre, Canberra, Ngunnawal Country, on 4 June, 2021, with the following cast:

| | |
|---|---|
| A | Roxanne McDonald |
| B | Katie Beckett |
| C | Dylan Van Den Berg |

Director, Ginny Savage
Set and Costume Design, Imogen Keen
Lighting Design, Gerry Corcoran
Sound Design, Peter Bailey
Set Build, Tony Theobold
Cultural Consultant, Gaye Doolan
Movement Cultural Consultant, Tammi Gissell
Production Manager, James Tighe
Stage Manager, Brittany Myers

## CHARACTERS

A, an Aboriginal woman from 1840s Tasmania.

B, an Aboriginal woman from 1960s Tasmania.

C, a fair-skinned, young Aboriginal man from the 2020s.

## SETTING

An island.

Even though they lived at different times, the ancestors communicate as though they're in the same space.

## NOTE

A group of Tasmanian Aboriginal people, many of them women, were removed from their Country and taken to the Bass Strait Islands in the early-to-mid 1800s.

They were sold, bartered and gifted as 'wives' to the white sealers who lived there.

For many years, it was said that the Palawa people were 'extinct'.

White history has swallowed our stories.

This is just one of many.

## 1. TINI DRINI (THE ISLAND OF THE DEAD)

*Lots of stones and rocks. Barren.*
*It's dark.*
*Suddenly—*
*A, B and C appear.*
*They're arranged like a family photograph.*
*They wait, looking for something.*
*Then—*
*A, B and C disappear.*
*And then sounds—*
*A girl tossing a stone into a river.*
*Whispers.*
*Wind.*
*A hymn, sung from far away.*
*Louder and wilder.*
*And then—*
*It stops.*
*Some silence.*
*We sit in this place.*
*Empty.*
*But brimming with something.*
*History?*
*The future?*
*Now?*
*C appears.*

C: Like a smack in the face. That's how I'd describe it.
  'I'm Aboriginal.'
  Maybe you're ticking a box at the dentist. Or telling the woman who works in the hospital emergency department.

'Oh, okay.'

You've got an idea of yourself and where you come from made up of whispers and jokes and other bits you've pulled together from somewhere.

And some people say it's not true and some people say it doesn't matter and some people say you look white anyway and some people say nothing.

You've got questions, not answers, just people frowning or eyebrows raised and front teeth biting down on lips and thin little voices and puffs of breath.

Don't want to say? Can't say? Don't actually know? *Do* know but it hurts too much to throw out the words—in case you actually hear them and have to come to terms with something?

What's there to come to terms with?

You hear it—you *say* it—and you only feel … I don't know.

So you go looking.

'No good comes from that!'

Why so many secrets? How can I ever know? Do I want to know? What does that change?

Questions questions questions.

And where did the uncertainty begin?

The root of it all?

You.

The thing that makes us ache and reach back restlessly for … something.

This all started with *you*.

And because I can't be a *full* person—like, filled up with the wholeness you might take for granted—I have to go looking.

And if you decide to do that—

You have to be prepared for where it might take you.

*The sounds of wind and whispers.*

*A hymn, no longer muffled, but getting closer and closer.*

You have to take a deep breath before you tell a story. Take a deep breath and make sure it's the one you *want* to tell.

Don't tell it before it's ready. Don't tell it before *you're* ready.

*More wind.*

*The kind of wind that could bend tree trunks in its wake.*

*Then—*

C *arrives somewhere.*

C *hears voices, slow and distant at first, but becoming sharper and more insistent—*

B: They already thought I was a bad mother.
A: Aim for the throat and wait.
B: You find out he's a two-timing rat—
A: They swoop in like eagles—
B: *Bad* mother—
A: God took two of 'em back—
B: You'll singe ya little fingers—
A: The end?
B: Sippin' on wine—
A: Is that the bad time?
B: Taste so good—

> A *sings.*
>
> *Louder.*
>
> *Harsher.*
>
> *Then—*
>
> A *and* B *appear.*
>
> B *prepares for a date.*
>
> A *collects stones and piles them up.*
>
> *She sings the hymn 'Trust and Obey'.*

A: [*singing*] Not a shadow can rise, not a cloud in the skies,
   But his smile quickly drives it away—
B: Really?
A: [*singing*] Not a doubt or a fear, not a sigh or a tear—
B: Got any Bee Gees?
A: Aye?
B: I'm goin' to the pub, not a funeral.
C: Where the fuck is this?

    B *notices* C.
B: Watch your mouth, boy.
    *Pause.*
  Who the fuck are you?
C: What?
    B *looks at* C *properly.*
B: Oh. You.
C: You know me? I mean—I know *you*—well, I *remember*—
B: Yeah. Hello.
    Pass me that brush.
C: Sorry?
B: It's for hair.
    A *notices* C.
A: You … Who are you? What do you want?
    A *brandishes a sharp stone.*
  You ain't from here!
B: It's alright, love. He's from down the line a bit.
    He's family.
C: Yeah. Family. From down the line.
    I know you, too.
    Well, *about* you.
A: You sure he's family, then?
    A *squints at* C.
B: Yeah, definitely family.
    Got his father's teeth. And his nose.
A: Got my eyes.
B: Got skinny arms.
C: Not *that* skinny—
B: And deaf like your great-grandmother. I said pass me that brush!
    C *passes* B *the brush.*
A: Ain't seen you 'round here before …
    A *looks at* C *again.*

My eyes aren't so good.
> Workin' against me. Can't always trust—

> A *looks around.*

Why am I here?
C: I … don't know.
B: I knew this was gonna happen. Can't even *die* and be left alone.
C: What is this place?
B: You better hurry up and figure it out. I've gotta go.
A: If you family, why don't I know you?
> You lyin'?
> Ain't no family of mine got skin like that—

> A *lunges at* C *with a stone.*

> C *escapes.*

You here to have ya way with us?
> Cut our throats?
B: Put ya rock down.
> He's family.
> I promise.
Could probably do with a whack on the head, though.
> Nosey bastard.

*Some wind.*

*Only* A *can hear it.*

A: Ssssh.

*Pause.*

You hear that?
B: No.
A: The wind?
C: I can't hear anything.
A: Listen! Wind will tell ya somethin'.
> Always there, always got somethin' to say.

> A *realises where she is.*

I know this place. This island.
C: An island?
A: They buried us here. Dents in the earth. Water all around us.

C: I'm ...
>    *We're* on an island?

>    B *claps her hands.*

B: Well done.
C: But where, exactly?
>    Like, which one?

B: Don't look like the Bahamas, does it?
C: Middle of the Bass Strait? Middle of ... somewhere?

>    *Pause.*

>    A *whispers to herself. It becomes louder and more urgent.*

A: There is there is there is there is there is ...
>    There is ...
>    There *is* ...

B: Hmm?
A: There is ...

>    A *tries to remember.*

C: There is ...?
B: Don't encourage her.
A: There is only one God!
C: Sorry?
A: There is.
B: Really?
A: Yes.
B: If you say so.
A: They told me there was only *one*.
B: I'll keep that in mind.
>    Shit. There's a hole—

>    B *notices a rip in her stockings.*

C: I guess it doesn't matter? Do you know—
A: What is the devil?
C: The devil?
B: Do any of you lot know how to sew?
A: You gotta get it right or you'll find yourself flat on your arse. What is the devil?

B: I dunno. The opposite of God?
A: The enemy of souls.
>And you—

>*A points at C.*

What is hell?
C: It's where all the bad people go.
A: Wrong! A place of torment.
B: Like this fucking island?
A: Watch ya mouth, girl!
>There *is* only one God. I hope to go to Heaven one day.

B: That's nice.
>You know how to stitch up a hole, don't ya?

A: I know about Heaven because of the … the … bible.
B: Oh? I haven't read that one.
A: It says that if I'm good, I'll get to go there.
C: You said you know this island?
A: The place where trees grow flat because of the wind—they look like they're lyin' down.

>*A seems unwell.*

I'll be gone soon.
C: You don't look well.
A: I got stories. I'm filled up with 'em. Gotta get 'em out before they're buried.

>*A speaks to the sky.*

Why'd ya bring me back to this place? You got a plan?
>I don't feel good.

C: Is she okay? Is there something we can do?
B: Nothing to be done.
>Ugh.
>You're both useless.
>I'll ditch the stockings.

A: He come for us one day—Maian Ginja. He come when it's time.
B: Not that this isn't a very interesting conversation, but what do you reckon— hair up or down?
C: Ummm. I dunno. Up?

B: I think I'll wear it down.

    I gotta go soon. I gotta look nice.

    She's gonna die. I'm goin' to the bistro. We're all goin' somewhere.

A: You're gonna leave me? Not here! Not this place!

    A *seems unwell again.*

    B *rolls her eyes.*

B: Sit down.

    Drink some water.

A: I used to be strong.

    B *feels a tinge of sympathy for* A.

B: You're strong. Still strong.

    *Pause.*

C: This island …

B: Hmm?

C: Why are we here?

B: All different reasons, I s'pose.

    *I* wouldn't be here if you didn't want to snoop about.

C: She's been here before?

A: They brought me here.

C: Where did you live? What did you eat? Looks like rocks and weeds and not much else.

B: You ain't gonna find a soufflé under a stone, mate.

A: There's always something if your belly needs it.

    That *man* used to holler at me when he was hungry.

    'Better have that bird stewin', woman, or I'll gut ya like a fish!'

C: You had a husband.

A: Ha! A husband!

B: Ha! I had one of those. He died.

    I didn't kill him, though. If that's what you're thinking.

C: He was a … strict man.

A: Made up his own rules. And fat! He was a fat man with hair on his back and breath like somethin' died in his throat.

B: My kind of bloke.

A: A white man. Used to try catchin' wallabies. He'd hide in the bushes and then BAM. He smash 'em so hard there'd be no animal left.

Came back with guts all over him, but no dinner. Without us black women, he woulda gone hungry. Maybe he wouldn'ta been so fat.

Us women caught the seals.

B: It was a job.

A: We brought 'em back home and the men would harvest the fur and the fat. Treated the carcasses like somethin' special. Better off bein' a dead seal than a black woman, that's what I reckon. They so gentle with the dead. They so tough on women with life still goin' on in us.

    A *tries to move.*

You gotta be patient—

B: You gotta stay there.

A: Listen!

    B *reluctantly helps* A.

A: You gotta be patient to catch one of them seals. Swim out to the rocks somewhere. Lie down, real quiet. Then you might see one come up, slippery from the water. It can't see you and it don't know it's about to die.

And you get close enough, and raise up your club—

    A *raises an invisible club.*

BANG!

    A *motions to* B.

Fall down like a seal.

B: What?

A: Fall down like I clubbed ya on the head and you a dead seal.

B: I gotta get ready—

A: Get yourself on the ground before I club ya for real!

    B *reluctantly becomes a dead seal on the ground.*

Or you could stab. Aim for the throat and wait. They made the saddest sounds. Like they wanted to tell you something but couldn't.

Then you carry it back to land.

    A *abandons* B *on the ground. She's too heavy.*

    A *finds* B*'s dress and it becomes a seal.*

B: Oi—that ain't cheap—

  A *drags the dress to another spot.*

A: Then you flip it over on its back.

  A *flips the dress.*

And slice right down the belly, through all the fat, all the way up to its throat.

  A *demonstrates.*

And you cut around the ribs. The blubber is good.

  A *sits, exhausted from the kill—but happy.*

You end up with a skin for dryin'. Then we sell 'em to men on boats.
 At the end of the day, all that's left is a pile of spines. Used up all the rest.

B: Can I get up now?

A: *We* knew how to do it best. We lived on 'em back on Country. Before this place. We did it with love. They did everything with money in their heads. Saw money in everything. The seals and the muttonbirds. The black women. The more you could kill, the more you were worth. If you bad at killin' … you better off dead.

B: That's men, eh. You gotta know how to work 'em. Then you'll be right. Like this bloke I'm goin' to see tonight—he said to me 'Sorry love, I only like blondes.' That's what he said. I tell him 'I'm a natural blonde, baby … this is just a dye-job. It'll fall out in a few weeks …' and next thing I know he's got his hands on some other woman but his eyes—they're on me. All night. And then he asks me out.

A: Small stuff make you feel like you still got life in you. Like spitting in his food.

  A *and* B *laugh.*

B: Or takin' a twenty out of his wallet when he goes for a piss.

A: Or fillin' your dress with dirt and gravel and leaves so he scrapes himself when he tries to get in.

B: Or sending letters to his *wife* when you find out he's a two-timing rat—letters with poems about his tiny dick.

A: Small stuff, eh.

B: I had a job too. A lot of different ones. I didn't kill anything—though I woulda been good at it. I drove taxis. All around the city. Blokes would sometimes get right back out again when they saw it was a woman driving, like I didn't know where I was goin'.
A: You got a job too?
C: Yeah, I guess. I'm still trying to figure it all out … but I write things.
B: Like what?
C: Lots of stuff. Stories and ideas that come to my head.
A: That's a job?
C: Yeah.

    A *and* B *laugh.*

I mean, I've done other things, too. Like, I cleaned a theatre, once. And I looked after kids a fair bit, and then after university—
B: Fancy shit.
C: Well, not really—
B: A long way from scrapin' oysters off rocks under the bridge. That's what I made you do.
C: I know. I remember.
B: That was honest work. None of this *university* shit.
C: It was unpaid. And I was five.
B: Ah, stop ya whingin'.
C: So, before the island—before all of this—what was it like?
A: You gonna write it down?

    A *laughs.*

    A *becomes unsteady and unwell.*

## 2. A SONG

A *is in another time and place.*

A *sings a lullaby to a baby.*

A: [*singing*] Goodbye to the sun
    My girl, my girl
    Goodbye to the creatures
    Who sing their own song.

Weep for the day
My girl, my girl
Weep for the birds
Who might lose their way.

Nana will go now
My girl, my girl
Dream of beauty
And not of the crow.

My ears will stay open
My girl, my girl
There's nothin' to fear
You're not on your own.

This song is for you
My girl, my girl
Keep it safe in your head
And sleep the night through.

   A *speaks to a baby.*

Sssshhhhh.
    You gotta sleep now, my girl.
    When you're dreamin', there's nothin' you can't see.
    Trees—fat and green from the rain.
    People dancin'.
    People smilin'. Cracks at the corner of their eyes, filled up with somethin'.
    Somethin' good.
    You can feel things when you're dreamin', too.
    And that's why we gotta sleep.
    'Cause there's nothin' better than a dream.

## 3. A LONG TIME AGO

C: A long time ago—

B: *Boring*—

C: Gran talked about the muttonbirds—about how they—

B: Got any jokes instead?

C: What?

B: The fella on the radio has jokes.

C: I don't. Sorry.

B: He was talking about how some government wants to send a ship or somethin' to space—well, to Mars—and it's gonna cost three billion dollars—and he said he can't believe we're gonna spend so much money lookin' for aliens—

Well, he didn't say aliens—he said *intelligent life*—

A *interrupts.*

A: Boy's tellin' a story.

B: What?

A: Let him keep talkin'!

B: I'm tellin' a joke—

A: Quiet!

A *motions to* C.

C: Umm. Yeah. So—

A: Muttonbirds.

C: Yeah.

That's it.

Umm. About how they all flew in at once—thousands and thousands of birds, and they turned the sky black. Sometimes the day might feel like night.

They tasted nice, Gran said. A long time after she left the island, she used to cook them out under the carport for Pa. She said they have a smell—when they're cooking. Something you notice. That's what she said.

B: And?

C: I'm just … talking.

B: Mum did that a lot. Cooked those birds.

C: Did you like the taste?

> *Pause.*

B: Don't remember.

> *Pause.*

C: So, before—
A: Before?
C: When you weren't on this island.
A: My home.
> I could follow the sky all the way back if I was young again.
> I wasn't lonely there.
>
> *Pause.*
>
> A *looks around.*

Happy, they said. We could be happy on this island. Ha!
> I need … to sit.
>
> B *helps* A *sit down.*
>
> A *remembers.*

A boy with a small face …
> He was seven. Is that right? Knocked over a gun and boom! Both his legs were exploded. Useless. Little pinstripe pants with holes and lots of blood. And we watched all the blood come out of him. It was a very long goodbye.
> Is that what I remember? Out of everything?
> I got the pants somewhere. Where are they?

B: I don't know.
A: I got 'em … somewhere.
> I just can't …
> I can't—
>
> A *is suddenly angry.*

You take 'em?
> You sneak away with 'em?
> Tell me where they are!
> I GOT 'EM SOMEWHERE!

C: We don't have them—we don't know where they are.
> But I'm sure we can find them. We can help you—

A: Enough. I'm tired.
   That … little boy …
   Maian Ginja …
C: Who?
A: Spirit. Brings death.
B: Only on his terms, though. If you're lucky.
C: Lucky?
B: Yeah.

> *Pause.*

> *A squints at C.*

A: I *do* know you … don't I? You like my husband?
   Got a young face. But still like him.
   What did you say—when you drink too much?
   You say …
B: A *lot* of things.

> *C becomes the Husband.*

C: You black women ain't got no idea!
   You black women ain't got nothin'. Ain't got nothin'!
   No idea about life off this island!

> *To C, with fury.*

A: But you ain't got no Dreaming … ain't got no … no love. For anything. Every morning I thank the trees for standing tall and the rocks for laying low. You thank nothin' or nobody. And when it don't give you what you want, you spit on it. Like that might help. You spit on me too when I did things you don't like. I couldn't dance. You allowed no dancing.

> *A cries.*

> *C is no longer the Husband.*

And now he's gone, but I can't dance no more.

> *A tries to dance, but cannot.*

C: I'm sorry that you couldn't …
B: I'm sorry too.

> *A lies down near the pile of stones.*

> A *counts the stones.*
>
> B *and* C *watch her.*
>
> B *prepares for her date.*

B: You ask a lot of questions.

C: I have more.

B: No doubt.
> Pass me that.
>> C *passes* B *an iron.*

C: Do you know who I am?

B: Yes. Grandkid. Something like that.

C: Your only one.

B: It's hard to keep track.

C: I was young when you died, so I don't remember much. Except—there was this thing you used to make. A dessert. You could make it in different colours. With packets of jelly and … cream or something?

B: Condensed milk.

C: Yeah.
> I liked it.
>> *Pause.*
>
> You don't … look like someone's nan.

B: Eh?

C: You're … not old?

B: Can be however old I like in this place.
> In this place, I'm goin' on a date.
>> *Pause.*

C: And she's your … great-grandmother?

B: Something like that.

C: I've heard a fair bit about her.

B: Good on ya.

C: I've heard a fair bit about *you*.

B: Here we go.

C: You … liked cheap wine.

B: The cheaper, the better.

C: You had cats.

B: I never turned a single one away.
I fed 'em. Loved 'em. Did what anyone would do.

> *Pause.*

> B *carries on preparing for her date.*

C: And what about her—who was that boy who died?

> *Pause.*

So you don't know?

> *Pause.*

A grandchild? A brother? A cousin?
And her husband? He died?
You said you knew this would happen. What'd you mean?

> *Pause.*

This place—this island ... there's no life.

> *Pause.*

What do you see here? If she sees it like a ... a graveyard—what do you see?

> *Pause.*

I see ... lots of stuff at once. Like, her. And you. Those worlds, plus mine, plus the descriptions I've read in books, plus the bits I've conjured up in my brain. Flinders Island. There's dry grass everywhere, but it grows sideways because of the wind. And the sea crashes against the rocks. And they're red—the rocks, I mean—like they're bleeding. When I turn away from the edge of the ocean, there's a mountain and I want to climb climb climb right to the top so I can look down and find the spots of ... sadness. The bits buried all over. Looks like it could be on a postcard, but there's something in the dirt and the air that just ... isn't as pretty. But it's also a place that ... I dunno ... that feels like it might belong to me? Like, the idea of it. Maybe?

> *Pause.*

B: Not worth thinkin' about.
C: It's just what I see.
B: Some things should remain as they are.

C: Stuck in time?
B: I didn't talk about it. Ever. Didn't need people knowing everything about us. We got off the island to get away from all that.
C: And forced yourself to forget.
B: My mother grew up on this island. Lived in a house made of flattened kerosene tins. Can you imagine the cold? Known for being black. Half-caste. They got off the island to rename themselves, and *tried not to remember.*
C: I *want* to remember.

> *Pause.*

B: Make us a cuppa, will ya.

> *Pause.*

C: Did you lie about it?
B: Water ain't gonna boil itself.

> *Pause.*

> B *straightens her hair.*

You gotta have smarts to straighten your hair. Ain't just anyone can make it smooth and silky.
C: Do you need help?
B: What? From you? You'd singe your soft little fingers.
C: I just—
B: This takes practice.
C: I'm sure—
B: There's some stuff they can't teach you at those fancy-arse schools.
C: Alright—
B: It's better if you're quiet.
C: Sorry.

> *Pause.*

I know she got taken away … and made to work. Passed around to those sealers like some kind of … I don't know. Her children—
B: They died. Two of 'em.
C: With her husband?
B: Yep. With the fat bloke. They were on a boat. Drowned. She never forgot. A lot of other things are gone from her mind, but not that.

C: So you ... *do* know things? Because Dad never said you did—he never said that—

    B *shrugs.*

B: And?
C: I'm not done—
B: I'm bored.
C: Why didn't you tell him?
B: I don't want to talk about your father.
C: Someone else did—someone felt like—
B: Look, I gotta get ready—
C: These aren't hard questions—
B: I didn't *say* they were hard—
C: Well, answer. Tell me.
B: I don't have to do anything. I mind my own business—
C: Burying stuff that happened is not 'minding' your business—
B: It is. It *is* minding because I didn't wanna get involved in it all.
C: Why? Why didn't you want to know?
B: For fuck's sake! We're different! Me? I gotta fit in. Don't want to be like her. You're lucky with that milky skin. You get no trouble. You get to carry it all on the inside—all the knowledge. Some of us gotta carry it on the outside for everyone to see.
C: Maybe that's right. Maybe I do look different. But don't we still come from the same place? Don't we still come—

    *Footsteps.*

    *Sound of a stick, dragging on the ground.*

    A *startles.*

A: Who's that? Who's that talkin'?
B: Ain't nobody. Go back to ya rocks.
A: I can hear him! I CAN HEAR HIM!
C: Who?
A: Get down, the both of ya.
    He's comin'.

    A *ushers* B *and* C *into a hiding spot.*

    A *whispers.*

Crunchin' along the path—stabbin' the ground with his stick.
Little man, but footsteps like he got bricks strapped to his feet.
Always hear him comin.'

C: What's his name?

A: Ssssh.
You hear?

C: A man from the island?

A: No … he come on a boat. From that other place. Told us about the Bible.
Taught us stories about heaven and hell. Told us they were the real places where spirits go. We told them about Tini Drini. The island where spirits live. Off in the ocean. You can never quite see it, but it's there. They said that spirits only go to heaven or hell. Heaven for being good. Hell for being bad.
What is a sinner?

B: Ummm—

A: You gotta get these right, you gotta remember—they test us. They line the children up outside the school and walk up and down and up and down and they ask us …

*C becomes the Priest.*

C: Who is the enemy of souls?

A: The devil!

C: Who was Abel?

A: Cain's brother!

C: What did Cain do?

A: Killed his brother!

C: And where did Cain go?

*Pause.*

A: He went to hell! Because he killed.

C: And killing is …?

*C is no longer the priest.*

A sin.

A: It's a sin.

*Pause.*

*Roxanne McDonald and Dylan Van Den Berg in The Street Theatre's* Milk, *2021 (Photo: Creswick Collective)*

C: You had to remember all this?

A: When the sun come up, we go to church. They teach us how to be better.

C: Better?

A: We learned as much as we could. We learned to find happiness in something we couldn't see. How else were we to be happy?

    A *resumes collecting stones and adding them to the pile.*

## 4. BLEEDING DAUGHTER

B *is in another time and place.*

B *holds a newspaper.*

B *gives advice to a teenage girl.*

B: I'm just gonna show ya somethin' real quick, my girl.

    See this? The personals. Most of the good lookin' blokes are off in Vietnam and I ain't the kind to write letters or wait patiently in my cardigan.

    But you gotta be careful. Lot of bullshittin' blokes out there.

    Like this fella—

    'Balding man, thirty-four, seeking beautiful young woman for stoking the fires on a rainy afternoon. Smoking preferred.'

    Mmmm.

    Firstly, no woman wants a man who's *honest* about his hair fallin' out.

    Get a comb, mate.

    Secondly, any bloke who uses a … a … fire … thing—like a metaphor, or whatever—ask your father, he'd know—any bloke who does that is a waste of time. All talk, but mostly fizzle when it comes down to it. Which it will.

    Nothin' about money, either. Be wary of that. Don't want to end up back at some bloke's place where he doesn't even have a wireless or a proper drinks cabinet.

    Next fella looks better—

    'Tall, athletic theology student (twenty-seven) looking for friendship and more (unavailable Sundays). Attractive woman sought for shopping, laughing, talking, etc.'

See? Like fuckin' poetry. This bloke knows what he wants. Has some cash. Gives you Sunday off.

He's not lookin' for some Suzy Homemaker—he's lookin' for me.

*Pause.*

You know what you're gettin', that's the thing about the papers.

Meet a bloke down the street? At the pub? Maybe he *looks* nice. Wearin' a squirt of cologne he bummed from the chemist. Padded out his wallet with bits of paper and old receipts to make him *look* like he can buy ya a seafood basket. And maybe you fall in love with him anyway. 'Cause he makes you feel … nice.

Back at his place one night.

You're woozy and thinkin' about havin' a spew.

'Been talkin' to a couple of people,' he says.

Oh yeah?

'Ain't you from that black family?'

Nah. Nah. I ain't.

He don't believe you.

Makes you own up to it with his fists.

'Black bitch.'

*Pause.*

So what I reckon is—

Stick to the papers.

## 5. SKELETONS

B: *I'm* happy. If you were wondering. Can I go now?
C: Where are you going?
B: Like I've been sayin', a date.
C: Now?
B: I'm gonna be late, thanks to you lot.
C: I'm sure they'll wait.
B: They *always* wait.
C: You go on a lot of dates?
B: You could say that. I've had a few blokes in my time. A fair few. Yeah. You could say I've done most of the blokes in Tasmania, if

you wanted. I don't give a shit about what anyone says. I hear 'em talkin' and I don't give a shit. Anyone who has a problem with it can get fucked. Just not by me.

C: And with some of them … do you ever fall in love?

B: Pfft. They like *me*. Love *me*, maybe. They all say I kept 'em around so they'd do stuff for me. Fix stuff, pay for stuff. Not wrong, I reckon. Not wrong. But I'm just tryin' to make it all work.

C: Did you love your husband?

B: As much as I could. Then he died. Left me with a kid.

C: I'm sorry.

B: It happens.

C: My grandfather.

B: That's right.

C: But not the *real* one.

B: Eh?

C: Dad heard it from the pantry. He was hiding in there, sneaking biscuits. You told some lady in the kitchen and that's how he found out. His dad wasn't his *real* dad. He was twelve. He stood so still, mouth full of choc-chips, afraid that even the smallest crunch would give him away.

    *Pause.*

    B *shrugs.*

    B *motions to* A.

B: Help me with my hair?
   He says up. I say down.

    A *helps style* B*'s hair.*

C: When were you going to tell him?

B: Eventually.

A: She didn't know how to tell him, that's what she reckons.

C: Because you lied about almost everything.

B: It's not lying if it's to a kid.

C: Right.

B: Look, he was a handsome man, your real grandfather. He coulda been in movies. He had a boat and he sailed down here and picked me up every weekend for a while. We ate oysters Kilpatrick on the deck and we had a lot to talk about.

There you go. The truth.

C: What was his name?

*Pause.*

B: Simon.

C: Simon?

B: Yep.

Worked at a bank.

C: Or was it Anton?

B: Anton?

C: From Czechoslovakia.

B: I don't even know where that place *is*.

C: Or John? A tall man from England. He sold used cars.

B: You're getting all mixed up.

Simon. Had a yacht. Worked at …

C: The bank.

B: The bank.

B *looks at her hair in the mirror.*

B: Do you think this is enough?

Let's spray.

A *uses hairspray. It's way too much.* B *likes it that way.*

And now my face.

A *helps* B *apply makeup.*

C: Do you ever tell the truth?

B: I don't reckon anybody does.

C *is frustrated.*

B *sighs.*

B *softens.*

You remember anything else? About me?

C: You?

Yeah.

I remember staying with you. And we went to lunch one day.

Drove down to the ferry and went across the water. Ate at the pub. I had chips or something. You had—

B: A nice moscato. Two or three, probably.

C: It was a nice day.

    I think of you whenever I'm back there.

    *Pause.*

B: Alright.

    Ask me something.

    *Pause.*

C: Why did you … hide or ignore or … I don't know. Why did you *lie* about …

    All of this. Why did you hide? That's my question.

B: I didn't hide it. I just didn't tell the truth.

    'Been up in Byron for a few months,' I'd say. 'Gettin' a bit of sun.'
    'My grandfather was from Malta.'
    'I'm a Thai princess.'
    I can be whatever I wanna be. That's what I reckon.

    *Pause.*

My aunty.

    Aunty Sarah. Every day she powdered her face and her arms to look more white. She couldn't visit her mother, couldn't risk people seeing her go into the house of a black woman.

    A *applies powder to* B*'s face.*

Not so much. Makes me look like a clown.

    There ain't much more to say.

    *Pause.*

C: Nothing else?

B: No. That's *all*.

C: You didn't tell Dad, then?

    *Pause.*

Never came up?

B: It was different.

C: Sure.

B: I didn't have any money. I didn't have *anything*. Except a kid.
C: And?
B: I didn't want to say. I didn't want to admit that I wasn't only poor and alone—
A: But also black.
B: When you don't know where the food is coming from … when you're doing whatever you can to keep things … going—you don't get to think about what came before.
C: It's not just what *came* before—it's about *now*—
B: You wanna make it significant. But it's just the past.

   *To* A.

   Sorry.

C: You know—
   I just want—
   Like, a *thing*—
   To hold onto.
   Something.
   Can't you just … give me that?
B: There's other stuff to worry about.
C: I don't understand you.

   B *shrugs*.

   *Pause.*

There's a picture of the family—a *real* picture. I've seen it. From the island. A bunch of kids sitting down the front. And right at the back, under some trees is a woman. Not so tall.
   It's her.
   It's real. It doesn't lie.

   *Pause.*

B: Do you reckon I need lashes?
   My eyes look naked. They gotta be dressed up a bit.
C: Don't you feel it? Whatever it is.

   C *motions to* A.

B: What do you *want* me to say?
   I'll say whatever you want.

C: It's about telling the story in the right way.
B: With your degrees and your fancy *words*.
A: Fancy Whitey words.

> A *and* B *laugh.*

> A *finishes* B*'s makeup.*

C: Tell me something else.

> *Pause.*

I get it. Things were tough.
B: Ha! You reckon?

I tried to … get out once. Closed up the kitchen with a towel along the bottom of the door. Drank some wine. Flicked on the gas and crawled into the oven, waiting to breathe it in and go to sleep.
A: But nothing happened.
B: Nah. The gas ran out. Too poor to die, apparently.

> *Pause.*

A: Maian Ginja wasn't ready.
B: He didn't come to me, even though I was screamin' out for him.

Can't trust men. Can't trust spirits.
C: I … didn't know.
B: Had your dad inside me. Things were shit.
A: No money.
B: Never any money.
A: And a baby.
B: A boy.
A: And so.
B: I tried to—

You know.
A: And here you are.
B: Here I am.

> *Pause.*

C: I'm sorry.
B: You're lucky.
C: I know.

> *Pause.*

A: Didn't ever cross my mind to do that. I always thought if I just waited, it'd come.
B: Wait long enough.
> I need my dress.

> *A brings her the dress.*

B: I'm gonna wear this and be beautiful.
A: Will you dance?
B: I s'pose I will.

> *Pause.*

A: I like to think about that. About you dancin'.
> I need to rest again.
> Sing me something.

> *B and C look to each other.*

C: I don't know what to … sing.
B: I don't feel like singing.
A: Then maybe some quiet.

> *Some silence.*

> *C begins to hum 'Amazing Grace'.*

> *He doesn't know anything else.*

> *B joins in, reluctantly.*

C: [*singing*] T'was … Grace that taught my heart to fear,
> And Grace—
> Ummm—
B: [*singing*] My fears relieved.
C: [*singing*] How precious did that Grace appear,
> The hour I first believed.

> *A falls asleep.*

C: She seems … so… peaceful.
B: She's dying.
C: Maybe that's why.
> Tell me something else. Please.

> *Pause.*

B: Pretty sure I'll come out with somethin' you don't wanna hear. Eventually.
C: I want to know all of it.
B: Alright.
> *Pause.*

I went to the pub with Mum once. And as we walked through the door, a young Aboriginal man stood and came over. He held it open for us and said, 'welcome Auntie.' Mum was embarrassed and we left.
C: Doesn't matter how much you try to forget?
B: Something like that.
> Alright.
> Now you.
C: Me?
B: Tell me something.
C: About …?
B: You.
> Jeez, thick as ya father.
C: I don't know what to tell you.
B: You happy? You got stuff that makes you get up in the morning? All that shit.
C: My life isn't like yours.
B: Lucky bastard.
C: Never missed out on anything.
> Good schools, good jobs, good everything.
> Still feel … unhappy. Sometimes.
> Sad.
> Well, more than sad, I guess.
> I—
> Thought about getting out, too.
B: But you're here.
> *Pause.*

Tell me something else.
C: Ummm.
> There was a—
> Like, a—

B: Spit it out.
C: Sorry—I just don't know what to—
B: Happiest you've ever been?
C: What?
B: Happiest you've ever been. Tell me.
C: Happy?
>*Happiest*?
>
>*Pause.*

   Sitting on a cricket pitch—
B: You play cricket?
C: No.
>God no.
>Just, on a cricket pitch. Middle of an oval.
>At night.

B: Alone?
C: No. Not alone.
>In the dark.
>In the quiet.
>It was just … nice.

B: What else?
C: Going to the movies. The dark bit at the start.
>Going to see 'Blue Poles' on a year-six excursion and thinking 'I could do that!'.
>Red wine. White wine. Sparkling wine.
>Getting married.

B: Married? How many times?
C: Just the once.
B: There's still time.
>*Pause.*

   And saddest you've ever been?
C: Sitting on my bedroom floor. Just wanted to … fold myself up and—
>Yeah.
>And then—
>The saddest?
>Saying goodbye.
>To you.

Sitting in a church.
An old lady playing the organ-thing and singing at the same time. You wouldn't have liked that.

*Pause.*

B: Fuck it.
I'm not going.

B *kicks off her heels.*

*She finds some wine.*

My mood's all gone to shit, anyway—thanks to you lot.

Poor bloke is gonna have a lonely night. Probably got his hair cut and everything.

Ah well.

*Pause.*

Get me a glass, would ya?

## 6. THE BIRD

C *is in another time and place.*

C *speaks to a young girl.*

C: You got a story for me?
No? You're not ready?
That's okay.

*Pause.*

We've got *lots* of stories. We've got stuff to tell.

I went up to Darwin for work once and ended up talking to a woman—an Elder. I told her that our mob have lost so much. She was quiet for a long time. And then she told me that we can find them all again—our stories, our Dreaming. We just need to go out and dance it all back.

Yep, dance.
And that's what I did.
I danced!

I went to the beach. I stomped through the water and spun around and around in the sand.

And a story leapt into my head.

For real!

It's about a bird.

The bird lived in a tree and each day he would sing a beautiful song and everyone would listen; the worms, the Tasmanian Tigers, the cockatoos.

Even the *bugs* would get up and dance.

Under the tree there was a Tasmanian Devil who lived in a cosy burrow.

She was young and it was her first winter. She had to leave home and search for food on her own.

'But how will I find my way back?' she asked.

The bird took pity on the little devil and said to her, 'No matter where you end up, listen out for my song and follow it back home.'

With that, the little devil headed off.

She was far, far from home—her belly full—when she decided it was time to turn back.

She closed her eyes and opened her ears and followed the bird's song.

But soon, the bird—weary from singing—lost his voice.

His song dried up in his throat.

The devil stopped in her tracks.

'How will I get home?'

She started walking in circles. The image of home she had locked up in her brain started to fade.

And then, a huge storm came—with rain and thunder and wind like nothing she'd seen before.

And on the wind—if she listened closely—she could hear the bird's song.

Soft. Far away. But there.

She started to follow the sound. Each time the wind blew, it carried the bird's song and the little devil crept closer and closer to home.

Until she—

*Pause.*

Tired now?

It's all out there.
Even the stuff we think is gone.
We just—
Have to listen.
We just—
Have to dance.

## 7. RIVER / SKY

B *is drinking.*

A *is sleeping.*

C *is thinking.*

B: I don't blame her, you know.
C: For what?
B: Wanting some quiet.
C: Yeah.
B: It's all I want, sometimes. To be left alone.

    *Pause.*

C: I wish I could walk exactly where she walked. What do you think the river sounded like where she came from? I have this idea—this theory—that rivers play their own, like, songs—
Maybe she'd think that's dumb.
B: Pretty dumb.
C: Do you reckon there was a certain smell that made her think: this is a happy time. Like when I wake up at Christmas? I wonder what her mother looked like? Did she teach her about the sky?

    And when she lost all of that … how did … I don't know … What did she do?

    *To* A.

If you could tell me … yeah. That'd be good.

## 8. THE TWILIGHT MAN

A *rises and dances.*
*It is beautiful.*
*Then—*
A *can't remember the dance.*
A *is disoriented.*
*Suddenly—*

A: I was dancin' when they came.
 They swoop in like eagles—but instead of claws they got big white arms, colour of bones.
 Never seen anything like it.
 I was a girl.
 Men rode in when it was dark—
 We feel the rumble of 'em coming before we see 'em.
 They struggled to cross the rivers—because they hadn't been out in those parts before.
 I know they comin' for me. And the others.
 The men try to fight.
 I lay so flat against the dirt I almost *become* it.
 Try to breathe real quiet.
 Don't move at all.
 But then—
 Screamin'.
 We run and run goin' whichever way we can—leaves and dust all around the place like a storm.
 And—
 They get me.
 Bundle me up.
 Put cloth in my mouth to stop me from yellin'.
 And they bring me to this place.

 A *tries to dance, like before.*
 *She's weary.*

*But she's desperate to hold on to the memory of moving her body—the joy, the pride.*

*It's too hard.*

C: None of this is *easy* to find out. You have to go looking.

B: No good comes from *that*.

C: Can't read *pain* from a book, I guess. Can't make you feel something when the truth is buried underneath the … the facts and the numbers and the *observations*.

But then sometimes you feel like you do know it. Like, all the cracks—they're filled up with stuff you didn't even know you had in your brain—or your heart or whichever bit.

If that makes sense?

Like, a thump in the chest. Comes from nowhere. But reminds you that you carry some of it too. You've got one hand that's gushing with blood, and in your other hand you're holding the knife.

You actually *are* the full story. Both sides.

A: No use gettin' worked up about it.

C: At school we learn so much about *other* places—*other* people.

A: It all makes sense when it's s'posed to.

*Pause.*

B: I dreamed of those other places.

A: Across the water?

C: Long way across.

B: I've been there. Once.

A: You went there on them boats?

B: Not boats. Can't stand boats.

Went on a plane—

A *is confused.*

C: Like a bird. Takes you wherever you want.

A: Must be a big bird.

B: I went to Austria. On a plane.

And I had a nice time.

C: I know this story.

You went to Austria because some man needed a wife—a *fake* one—

B: Fake? It was real. For a few weeks. As far as his folks knew, anyway.
C: You answered an ad in the newspaper.
B: 'Want to see the world? Just gotta be my wife for a fortnight.'
>Thought it was too good—*way* too good.
>But it was real.
>He lied to his folks—said he was married to some Australian lady. So when he went home, had to take proof, didn't he?
>Sometimes we gotta tell stories like that. Made sense to me.

A: Glad I'm not a bird, takin' the both of you all that way.
C: You left Dad on his own for a few weeks. Stacked up a pile of videos, sent someone round to feed him—
B: Him *and* the cats—
C: Left him there *like* a cat.
B: A twelve-year-old boy ain't a *kid*.
>You could be put to work at that age.
>He was fine.

C: What were you getting away from?
B: What's that supposed to mean?

>*Pause.*

>It was a nice place. Austria. Snowed a fair bit. Liked that part.

>*Pause.*

>I don't regret doin' anything. Just got to say that.

C: Not a single thing?
B: No. Nothing.
C: Taking his money?
B: I *spent* it—to keep wheels turning in our shit hole—
C: Running off every weekend—
B: I *lived*—
C: Must've been lonely. For him.

>*Pause.*

B: Yeah. Lonely.

>*Pause.*

>He moved in when we got back. The Austrian.
>Good to have a man in the house for a bit.
>He wasn't so bad.

A: If a man keep to himself, he ain't so bad.

No good havin' him up in your face all the time. Get to feel tired from that.
B: Maybe you like him, though. Maybe you don't mind if you *like* him.
A: Eh. Not many to like.
C: No-one else on the island?
A: We all spread out.

*Pause.*

There was one.
B: Ha! There's *always* one.
A: Liked the look of him.
B: A woman knows what she wants.
A: 'Cos even though I got a husband, he send me off sometimes. To the other blokes.

And this one …

He took me a few times. Treated me like shit when we were out in the camp. Barely looked at me. Put me to work.

But at night—
B: At night, eh?
A: A sweet man. Lay me flat and rubbed my legs and back—sore from workin'. Make me feel good.
B: I bet he did.
A: Maybe there are other men like him. With gentle hands and soft words.

But the fat man always take me back.

Dunno how little boys with big hearts grow up to be men with big holes in their chests. Somethin' happens.

My *husband*.

I think he will be in hell. Which is funny.

A *laughs.*

When he climbed up on me, I used to wish I could send him there.

Used to whisper stuff in my ear, about how he hated me. About how he wanted me. Like he couldn't make up his mind.

A *stares at the rock in her hand.*

B: I wouldn't put up with that shit. Don't whisper in my ear, mate.
A: I had a plan. I thought about it most nights. About gettin' up quietly—

B: Because you haven't been sleeping—
A: About finding him outside—
B: 'Cos you locked the bastard out.
A: Put a wooden chest up against the door.
B: He can shove and holler all he wants, but he ain't getting in.
A: He's too drunk to do anything 'cept fall asleep in the dirt, up against the tin walls.
B: Serves him right.
A: He's breathin' real heavy, making his belly go up and down and up and down—
B: Fat bastard.
A: And I wonder if it might stop—
B: Round and fleshy and hairy—
A: With no more air.
    I've got a rock in my hand. Been holding it all day.
B: Don't be scared. He deserves it.
A: I think about—
B: Don't think about nothin', just get it done.
A: Heaven. Prayers. Nasty words.
B: Think on heaven later.
A: I raise the rock—
B: Yes!
A: And I smash it down—
B: Bang!
A: Bang!
B: Bang!
A: Again—
B: And again—
A: And again.
B: He wakes for a moment and feels it. Really fucking *feels* it.
A: I don't even smile.
B: I would. I would smile. Laugh in his face.
    *Pause.*
A: He's dead. And it's quiet. Maybe I hear some waves in the background.
B: Walk outside and put the rock back in the dirt—
A: Where it belongs.

*Pause.*

But I didn't wanna go to hell with him. So I did nothin'.

B: You fucked up.

A: I missed the chance.

B: Because he drowned. The fucker fell off his boat. Gulped water into his lungs and sank like a stone.

A: Swallowed up by the ocean he robbed. Taking two of my babies with him. Is that the cost for a bit of silence? A moment to breathe?

*Pause.*

Am I goin' … to that place? Hell?

*Pause.*

C: You won't go there. You won't see him again.

*Pause.*

B: Happy now?

C: What?

B: Got what you needed?

C: I—

B: Your skin's a ticket outta this place.

C: How can I just throw it all away?

B: All the ugly bits are yours as well.

The fat fella? Her husband?

Your blood's all muddied up with him too.

A *is upset.*

A: Blood? Why you talkin' about blood?

B: You know.

A: No … I—I don't.

C: What are you talking about?

B: You really wanna know?

C: I mean, it's not—

B: No no no—you gotta hear it.

Would be *easier* if we skipped this bit.

C: She's tired. *I'm* tired—

B: Come on. You think that bloke was bad? She ain't much better. None of us are.

A: I need to …
B: You gonna tell him?
C: What?
B: Easy to think *I* did all the shit stuff.
A: No no no no no.
>    I don't *feel* good.
>    I don't feel—
B: Tell him about the babies.
A: Babies.
>    I got babies.
>    Where are they?
>    You seen 'em?
B: What did you do to 'em?
C: Leave her alone. She's—she's not well.
A: Me? I … I didn't do …
B: The first two. The first two babies that fell out of you on this island—where are they now?
C: No—you can stop.
>    Look at her!
>    Look what you're doing!
B: Now you wanna stop?
>    Oi. Where are the babies?
>    WHERE ARE THEY?
C: STOP!

>    A *looks around.*

>    A *points to the stones.*

A: They … they … *here*.
C: You can sit down—you don't need to—
B: Do you reckon they cried?
C: Enough—
A: Cried? No. They didn't cry …
C: Don't listen to her—
B: Did they know what was goin' on?
A: I gotta sit down—
C: You *need* to stop.
B: Can't stop now, too far in—

C: Leave her alone!
B: Worried about her? Or worried about *you*?
C: Please.
> Can't we let her just … keep it?
> Like, whatever it is.
> Let it be hers.
B: She's gotta say it.
> She'll keep on sayin' it.

*Pause.*

A *is distraught near the pile of stones.*

A: The babies.
B: The babies.
A: I …
B: She killed 'em.

*Pause.*

She killed her own babies because they were white.

*Silence.*

*Not a breath from anyone.*

A: I ain't never seen a white man before. I thought they came out of the sea, came out of there to take me away.
B: And you didn't want 'em growing inside.
A: White man everywhere, now he inside me too.
> When they came out, they didn't cry.
> They look more like him than they look like me.
B: But that didn't matter.
A: No. They still seen as scum by white man.
B: Seen as scum by you.

A *moves towards* C.

A: Not straight away. I looked at 'em.
> Soft skin. Different color to mine.
> Little eyes open …

A *looks into* C*'s eyes.*

They look like you!

A *grabs* C*'s throat.*

C: It's me.
>It's *me*.
>I'm not—

A: YOU!
>The man who take me away.
>The man who get on me every night.
>Put himself inside me.
>Grew himself inside me.
>Then came out of me, not cryin', not lookin' the right way.
>So I took all the air out of 'em.
>
>A *puts more pressure on* C*'s throat.*

I do it quickly.
>I do it outta love.
>I do it *with* love.
>
>A *lets go of* C.
>
>C *breathes again.*
>
>A *nurses* C.

The other women—they see me do it but they do nothin', fear of God in their eyes.
>I do it twice. I hide 'em away and tell my husband—

B: 'Born without life in 'em.'

A: That's what I say.

B: He shrugs.

A: But the third time, another woman take him away so fast I can't do nothin'. Stuck with a baby boy. Fourth, fifth, sixth, seventh. I got a whole lot of 'em.
>God took two back for what I did. That's what I paid.
>I hope He's good to 'em. Put 'em in a nice place.
>I reckon God's got a riverbank where he send all the children. Babies float down for ever and ever in tiny baskets. Kids throw rocks and swing from trees. It goes on and on and there's no work or yellin'.
>I got three left. Filled 'em up with stories.
>Learned to love them all.
>And they learned to love me back.

> A *strokes* C's *hair.*

And I got you, eh?

C: The stories stopped here. They almost didn't go any further.

> C *points to* B.

A: I was scared of that. You die knowin' what white man has done—but not knowin' what he's gonna do next.

C: You knew all of this?

> *Pause.*

B: Look—

> My mother—
> Yes.

C: Never felt the need to say? Never thought that anyone would care?

B: You don't get it.

C: I don't. I really don't. I thought I knew you. I thought that all the stories and bits and pieces would amount to a sense of you. But right now? You seem more like a stranger than you were to start with.

> *Pause.*

Tell me why you never said it.

B: I don't—

C: Just tell me.

B: Watch your tone, boy.

C: Tell me!

B: No—

C: TELL ME!

> *Pause.*

Just ... try.

B: I didn't say it. Because.

> I didn't say it because I didn't want us to get found out.
>
> I didn't say it because if people knew, we could have our windows smashed in.
>
> I didn't say it because the government already thought I was a shit mother.
>
> I didn't say it because my father *did* say. And when he got back from the war, where he could've died, they didn't give him *nothin'*.

I didn't say it because there are always promises promises promises.

I didn't say it so it could be better.

*Pause.*

C: That's.
I just—
I'm sorry.
You know, there's no shame.
We still talk about you.
Hard to forget.

*Pause.*

B: I should have—
Yeah.
All this.
I'm—
You know that?

C: But it didn't stop.

*Pause.*

A: The stories. You got 'em now.

C: Yeah.
I want to know all of this for what comes next.
I want to write it down because I've got a baby coming.
A girl.
And I want *her* to know all of it.
Even though she won't look like you—or you.
She'll have the knowledge.
Because I'll whisper it in her ear and she'll know where she came from and *who* she came from.
It won't stop. Not again.

*Pause.*

A: A baby.
B: A girl.
A: Don't you let go!
B: Hold her the right way—

A: With your hand under the head.
B: If she cries—
A: She's hungry.
B: Or bored.
A: Or tired.
B: Rock her gently—
A: She'll sleep.
B: Rub some whiskey on her gums.
A: Or sing.
B: And if any man ever think he's *big*—
A: And *mighty*—
B: And try to be king shit—
A: With his *words* and his *fists*—
B: She don't have to hang around—
A: 'Cos he ain't got no business tryin' to love her.

> A *and* B *are surprised.*
>
> *Pause.*

C: Thank you.

> *Pause.*
>
> A *falters. She is unwell.*
>
> B *sits with* A.
>
> *There's a moment.*

B: You can go now.
    We both can.
A: Now?

> A *looks around.*

  Where am I goin'?

> *Pause.*

C: You're going home?

> A *shrugs.*

A: I would like to go home, but they say God has plans for us. He made this one for me.
C: White men have plans.

A: Come.
>   Let's pray.
B: Do I have to?
C: I don't really know how.
A: Close your eyes.
>   *They close their eyes.*

  Our Father.
B: Our Father …
C: Up there in … heaven
B: Right.
A: Hallowed be thy name.
B: This is hard—
C: Thy kingdom—
B: Kingdom?
C: Come.
A: Thy will be done.
B: Don't think so, mate.
C: Here on Earth—
A: Give us bread.
B: Every day, thanks.
A: Lead us not—
C: Into temptation—
B: Sorry boys, can't be led!
A: Deliver us from evil—
B: From evil—
C: From evil.
A: And forgive us.
B: Yes please!
A: Amen.
B: Amen.
C: Amen.
>   *Pause.*

  And now—
A: We die.
B: Both of us.
A: Outside. On the ground with my children.

B: At the dinner table. I smash one of the good glasses.
C: Were you afraid?
A: No.
C: Does it hurt?
B: No.

> Sippin' on wine. Taste so good. Feel something going on inside but don't give it any attention. Then it all swirls around. And off I go.

A: Is *that* the bad time? When it stops?

> *A laughs.*

> Eyes ... closed. No needles of light.
> Black.
> Heart going ba-boom ba-boom ba-boom 'til it stop.
> The stink of dirt and muck—then that gone too.
> And then—last of all—my ears.
> They go last.
> And I hear ... What?
> My boys? Yelling yelling yelling from too far out?
> No.
> He don't give me that. God don't give me a prayer, whispered close for comfort. He don't give me sounds of the furnace where them bad people go.
> What He give me—at the end—right before it all stops—
> Quiet.

B: Quiet.
A: He give me that.

> At last He give me that.

> *Some silence.*

> *Then—*

> A, B *and* C *pose for a family photo.*

> A *disappears.*

> *Then—*

> B *disappears.*

> C *is left alone.*

> *He looks at his hands.*

*He picks up a stone.*
*He puts it in his pocket.*
*He looks far away.*
*And then—*
*Blackout.*

END

www.ingramcontent.com/pod-product-compliance
Lightning Source LLC
Chambersburg PA
CBHW040055100426
**42734CB00044B/3427**